Celebrate ~your~ womanhood Therapy

Celebrate-your-womanhood Therapy

written by
Karen Katafiasz

illustrated by
R.W. Alley

ONE
CARING
PLACE
Abbey Press

Text © 1992 Karen Katafiasz
Illustrations © 1992 St. Meinrad Archabbey
Published by One Caring Place
Abbey Press
St. Meinrad, Indiana 47577

Library of Congress Catalog Number
92-73664

ISBN 0-87029-254-4

Printed in the United States of America

Foreword

In a study not long ago, girls said that being a boy would make their lives better; boys had contempt for the idea of being a girl. Centuries of cultural attitudes devaluing women have left their legacy. Many women continue to feel a vague emptiness within, a doubt that they are fully adequate and acceptable.

Through history, women's "place" has usually been clearly defined, with certain roles reserved for males. Women who challenged the restrictions often found success by being as much like men as possible. To think or act "like a man" was considered high praise.

But women realized that shattering old constraints under these terms required them to abandon something of incomparable value: the richness of their own life experiences and ways of being.

Women's identity does not depend on measuring up to men, as if maleness were the standard for humanity. Nor are women's experiences just a footnote to the "real" story of men's history. Rather, women's and men's lives stand parallel, side by side, as equally valid and valuable ways of being human.

Using the lighthearted "elf-help" style, this book presents a healthy alternative to the toxicity of sexism, as it celebrates the power, the pride, the glorious possibilities of womanhood.

1.

Stand proudly and exult in your
womanhood. Remember:
Women hold up half the sky.

2.

Women in your family who have come before you have left legacies of strength, humor, endurance, unconditional love. Join your spirit with theirs and claim their legacies.

3.

Remember your foremothers in the history of the human family. Their brave struggles for justice and change have paved the way before you. You can claim their legacies too.

4.

In many early human communities, women were the primary food providers, builders, artisans, healers, leaders, as well as the creators of life. Feel your connectedness to those women; recognize your rootedness in them.

5.

Your way of leading may be different from how you see male leaders function. That doesn't make you wrong; you bring something of value. See how you can integrate the best of both styles.

6.

Know that your way of
being human is as valid and
significant as a man's. Women
are not a subspecies in the
human race; women are not an
auxiliary for the men's club.

7.

It is good to experience life
in a woman's body. You don't
have to use all your body's
capabilities to be amazed and
grateful for its possibilities.

8.

Don't allow ignorance, fears, or insecurities to define what women should be or can do. Challenge limitations that are imposed and false; transcend them.

9.

Support and encourage women (including yourself!) who want to test their abilities in nontraditional roles. Applaud women who blaze new paths.

10.

Live "both/and," not "either/or."
You can make a cake <u>and</u> make a
deal, push a baby carriage <u>and</u>
push for justice. (But that
doesn't mean you have
to do everything.)

11.

Proudly claim the word "woman." That clearly names the adult that is you, the adult who can effectively care for the "girl" who is inside you.

12.

Rejoice in your deep connection
to the rhythms of the universe.
Your monthly cycles are as
wondrous a part of the
cosmos as the tides and the
phases of the moon.

13.

There is a natural wisdom in your life's cyclic pattern—your experience of shedding the old and regeneration, of fullness and emptiness, of rest and activity. Let it teach you.

14.

When a man offers you a
courtesy, acknowledge his action
as one human being to another.
You can hold the door open for a
man or another woman if it's the
considerate thing to do.

15.

Cherish the beauty and art in "traditional" women's crafts like quilting, knitting, sewing, weaving. They are priceless expressions of creativity and talent.

16.

Be about the birthing process
in all aspects of your life.
Consciously "give birth" in your
family, your relationships,
your work, your art.

17.

You have within you a strength
that is the full expression of your
womanliness. Draw on it;
depend on it.

18.

It's fine to want to look attractive. But it feels best when you do what seems natural, not phony, and when you start, not from a position of self-hate and insecurity, but from one of self-love and acceptance.

19.

Your ability to make connections, nurture relationships, value life is a gift. Apply it to your community; exercise it globally.

20.

When you are demeaned,
diminished, or dismissed, assert
your dignity with conviction.
You can do so without
demeaning the other person.

21.

Refuse to be exploited, patronized, or treated as an inferior, an accessory, an ornament. Feel a solidarity with other women when they are. And do what you can to bring about change.

22.

There's no need to wait for Prince Charming — or for anyone else who will take care of you and your life. You can make decisions, assume the initiative, shape your existence, take responsibility for yourself.

23.

Rejoice in your abilities. When you do something well, it's not "just like a man" or "pretty good, for a woman." It's womanly and it's <u>you</u>.

24.

No other person can make
you feel whole. Your wholeness
comes from an inner peace
and integrity—your feelings,
beliefs, principles, actions,
all in harmony.

25.

Treasure and care for yourself and then you can treasure and care for others. Your love will flow out to others without the restrictions of your own neediness and hidden agendas only when you fill up yourself first.

26.

You are an embodiment of the sacred, an exquisite image of God, who birthed us, nourishes us, continues to nurture us.

27.

Experience your sisterhood
with other women.
You share journeys, hurts,
yearnings, joys in ways
deeper, more essential,
than disagreements
and competitiveness.

28.

Experience the common humanity you share with men. Enjoy the differences and the similarities you each bring to relationships.

29.

Respect your intuitive knowledge. It is emotional wisdom and razor-edged logic working together.

30.

With awareness, you can
transform everyday tasks
into the sacred. A housekeeping
chore becomes a transcendent
ritual creating a place of
warmth, safety, and peace for
yourself and others.

31.

You hold within you the reconciling of opposites, the integration of dualisms: You are both mind and body, earth and spirit, emotion and reason, light and dark, receptivity and action, vulnerability and strength, female and male, dying and rebirth.

32.

You have the power of co-creation. Explore the ways you can exercise power <u>for</u>, not power <u>over</u>.

33.

Accept and experience the grace in growing older. Character and wisdom are beauty.

34.

Experience self-acceptance deep within, in every part of your body, mind, spirit. Be at ease; you have a right to your place in the universe.